The Hunter

BOOKS BY GEORGE MURRAY

Carousel: A Book of Second Thoughts (2000)
The Cottage Builder's Letter (2001)
The Hunter (2003)

The Hunter

Smoke not Clouds, Sunset not Flame

GEORGE MURRAY

NATIONAL LIBRARY OF CANADA CATALOGUING IN PUBLICATION

Murray, George, 1971-
The hunter / George Murray.

Poems.
ISBN 0-7710-6675-9

I. Title.

PS8576.U6814H86 2003   C811'.6   C2002-905225-4

We acknowledge the financial support of the Government of Canada through the Book Publishing Industry Development Program and that of the Government of Ontario through the Ontario Media Development Corporation's Ontario Book Initiative. We further acknowledge the support of the Canada Council for the Arts and the Ontario Arts Council for our publishing program.

The epigraph from Albert Camus is from *The Fall*. Copyright © 1956 by Alfred A. Knopf, Inc. Reprinted by permission of Vintage Books, a division of Random House, Inc., New York.

The epigraph from A.F. Moritz is taken from the poem "Foundation" from *Between the Root and the Flower* by A.F. Moritz. Copyright © 1982 by A.F. Moritz. Reprinted by permission of the author.

Typeset in Aldus by M&S, Toronto
Printed and bound in Canada

McClelland & Stewart Ltd.
The Canadian Publishers
481 University Avenue
Toronto, Ontario
M5G 2E9
www.mcclelland.com

1 2 3 4 5   07 06 05 04 03

For Ailsa . . .

Do not wait for the last judgement, it takes place every day.
– Albert Camus

Noon is a kind of dusk.
– A.F. Moritz

HUNTER

The forest lies quiet immediately before the axe,
the desert gives up accelerating the wind.

Across the earth game birds and salmon go still,
deer and bison and hoary goats freeze instantly.

It is he who stepped on a lizard's throat and called it
a dragon, he who defeated a mountain village

and named it a kingdom, he who hung for a night
and bled song from his wounds, he who chases

the chariot sun across the sky and never catches it.
Let us retreat to a time of less and more sin, he says.

Let us entreat our wives and sisters to birth monsters,
let us return to the roots of our earliest prophecies.

As a fisherman he has cast his line over and again into
the sea, coming away with only Gilgamesh, Jonah,

Grendel. As a farmer he has set innumerable seeds
and nuts into runnels of earth and has only managed

to grow Nefertiti, Helen, Guinevere. As a hunter
he has run his knife between the ribs of countless ermines,

grizzlies, and blue foxes, yet has never spilled
a drop of blood that wasn't that of Pythagoras,

Ptolemy, Copernicus. He is a man who would tip
the earth, sip from the edge of a continent

as though the sea bed were the bowl of a goblet.
Reincarnation, he tells us when we beg,

was removed from the list of reasons not to kill
when we reached the point of more people

alive on the planet than have ever lived
and died in all of history and story. He moves

among us on his beasts, he travels the boar-runs
of the forest without the slightest snap

of twig or branch, he walks across the waters
of our moats and seas, slides between the cracks

in our windowsills, lifts the sheets of our beds,
climbs our bodies to the throat

and lets loose springs of life to course down
the topography of our testament to living.

It is he who stands squinting into the blowing dust
and sand as though tired after a long chase,

he who looks upon us fondly as though
recently given over to love after years spent

in doubt, he who raises the standard
that bears an emblem none of us expected.

For consolation he tells of the buzzard
that has lit on his shoulder where a falcon should,

how he's forced to remind it constantly
with a mailed fist that he is still alive,

just barely. *In this world,* he says, *everything will be
claimed by the sand. In this world we are*

*always wandering the desert. In this world the desert
is the Promised Land. In this world the Promised Land*

is still just over the horizon. In this world, he says,
drawing a blue blade with a shriek that runs shivers

up and down the mountainsides,
the horizon is what you see when you look up.

Valley

So far. We are so far out from everything
the mules cannot go on, the camels
are landing chin-first in the dust.

So far our stores are reduced
to rinds and crumbs,
so far our meagrely dressed guide

long ago turned back
to the thick air of her jungle cave.
Who could have guessed

we would be the hardy ones?
Who would have thought
it would be us cresting

the rocky hills, parting the underbrush
with long knives,
sluicing over the final waterfalls?

Our bodies fall headlong
into another undiscovered valley
where the only things

familiar that await our coming
are the stars, disease,
roaches, and the bones of our guide.

Ruins

What once stood here? Ruins.
The remains of a city?
No, just ruins. The remains

of a temple or home? No, just a shell.
As that of an egg?
As that of an insect. Was what

once stood here something
that fell into disrepair?
Everything is as it was. Is it

the same as it always has been
despite the rising tide
of time around its ankles?

It forgot about time shortly
after time began.
Then what once stood here

does not know time?
It acknowledges
its existence. It defies time?

It cannot comprehend it. It blocks
the passage of time?
Yes, but it is time's only path.

You would have us call it ruins?
It is only what once
stood here. How then was

that which once stood here
made if not with
the assistance of time? It was built.

Chain

The first horseman to wander into this valley
was once again mistaken for a monster:

his thoughts were broken, his body split, not as
a tree might be in a storm but as a couple

might unexpectedly after twenty years. It's good
to see the apples have completed their cycle,

green to red to black, sour to sweet to bitter,
proof the world goes on in pieces

uninterrupted. A man on an empty street corner
is the first to be seen in days and all he has

to say is that the Garden of Earthly Delights
is covered in dirt. Imagine! Volcanoes

go off as though they were stew
left too long on the stove.

The seismic spike recorded on paper
is wholly different from that recorded in earth.

Are you confident enough to say definitively
these earthquakes are not of Biblical proportions?

Scattered about the country are signposts
to towns that no longer exist.

The water refuses to run in expected directions,
machines will not vend their hoards of candy

and soda, squirrels and mice are giving lip
to old ladies on benches, starlings

are committing acts of fraud in the very trees
above. There is not a lick of shade left

in Coventry, not a grain of sand in Cairo.
The kilns of this world have no walls,

yet still they cook, the ovens have no elements
and the hearths no chimneys,

yet everything smokes!
Five Christ-figures stand in a police lineup

and those behind the bulletproof glass
are hard-pressed to pick even one;

someone mentions acidly that the only memorable
conversation at the Last Supper

was about the amount of salt in the soup.
That day when the hydrants decided to withhold

their water and ignored our requests
to douse the nearby fires was the same day

the only city on the planet that didn't burn
was Atlantis. Half-naked is half more clothed

than we need for what is to be done;
dress yourself in the costume of a Greek athlete

instead of the torn garb of a Sabine woman.
When we walk through the victory arch,

so prematurely built, we will die
and be born at the same time;

as with any door, the person going in
is not the one coming out. Any good Centaur

knows there's a chance he'll·be mistaken
for a horseman cresting the ridge,

so when the road forks beneath you, wisdom
dictates you take the third route, that leading home.

Take a look around when you reach the horizon.
A chain dangles from the sun. Tug on it.

WEATHERVANE

The weather has suddenly become inarticulate,
unable to confess its own crimes,
much less finger those who abused it.

It is time to parent the monsters of this world,
time to police the rabbits and hamsters, it is time
to execute the innocents in ingenious machines.

Does no one else feel it? The pressure?
The unease? There have been predictions
of a whole lot of an unspecified something

for quite some time. The continents
are as moody as a life raft lost deep at sea,
the passengers as excited and hopeless as well.

During the good weather a wasp gets caught between
the panes of a window; everyone in the room
is safe from its sting, but still uncomfortable.

Perhaps, as the wasp looks for a way out
of a trap that was never set and cannot be seen,
people can't help concluding

things are going undone, purposes unfulfilled.
If life keeps getting better, then it should always
be the best (or so logic dictates), but nothing

is so memorable it can't be forgotten.
In the worst weather, while God ignored
Noah's polite *when* and poured down the flood

as though it were hot tea over the back
of a hand, the weathervanes of the world
were repeatedly rusted still and torn free.

Look there, it still shakes a negative,
a panicked indecision, its shape one moment
a crowing rooster, or pointing dog,

or human palm, the next a pile of dust blowing
away beneath a lightning rod. The house,
strangely quiet, is suddenly unable to foretell

weather in anything but the most immediate fashion.

WALL

The mists at the edge of the world
have been pushed to the end of their patience

and are now rebelling, have become solid
and thick as a retaining wall, have encroached.

Protect your children! the poster reads.
Put your shoulder into it, heave, lash out!

Your reluctance to enter the vapour
is each brick, your reticence to acknowledge

its existence and the extent of our defeat
is the mortar that holds it together.

There is a number so large it cannot be
written on a single sheet of paper

and when it is seen it can only be held
in the mind for a moment before it crumbles

to its separate component integers.
A man separates from a small crowd

and makes his way towards another, selling
finger bones, femurs, and skulls;

there is a trade in human remains that has yet
to be explained to anyone's satisfaction.

He has almost collected an entire hand.
Below every molecule of water in the ocean

there is a desert and below that is another water
that separates humanity's feet from the fire.

Imperceptibly, the rock is still smouldering.
Minutely, the meteors are raining down.

Violin

Here is a mildly frightening thought:
most representations
of Hell have a sky. If only we could

alert whoever parents the gods
that their cruel children
have somehow obtained matches

and a magnifying glass. A bomb
in the stroller, mustard gas
and snakes in the can of soda,

a foreign-language luminary in the back
of the limousine:
these are the things it will kill us

to see. The statues that line the paths
of the campus where
children are trained to be prodigies

need a good massage, need to learn
how to loosen up.
Were every child given a violin

and set before the royalty of Europe,
would there still be
royalty? Which young one was it

who asked the professor: *If Heaven is
the opposite of Hell,
does that mean they will forever be*

dousing your intestines with water, applying
strips of skin to your tongue,
regurgitating your organs, doing work

for you? Only now are the strangers
getting the point of it:
it's dangerous to talk to children.

Stage

We are a welcome mat for the gods.
The margin of error grows
more generous each day. The margin of Eros . . .

How is it, again, that we think this one particular
crucifixion proved anything
about immortality? It's time to think

the unthinkable and store our celebrities
in cool trailers against an age when
no one will be famous, against a time

when fame will be outdated. Are we ready to call
our killers artists? They are very good
at what they do, after all. We live in a society

that uses fresh water to catch and transport feces,
a society that shits in
perfectly serviceable water. Is it any wonder

that the rest of the planet despises us?
Suddenly the brunch crowd
is talking about things other than the price

of rent, other than Henry's latest beheaded wife,
other than the Who's Who of this week's
listings in the Bubonic White Pages. Suddenly

the salons are full of jabber about the roots
of Arthurian legend, about
what constitutes responsible punishment

for Roman soldiers, about the likelihood
of ever finding the lost plays
of Sophocles. When will the gods

find themselves unexpectedly conspicuous
once again? How difficult is it
to wake from a dream in which you can't remember

your lines and find yourself smack on stage?
O Gilgamesh, dear old friend,
what would you have to say about this filthy flood?

Look at that idiot, Love, you'd say, he's wearing
such a lost look. It should really be
on the face of that fellow in Babylon,

the one who has just fallen
from a mountainside
                        and has yet to hit the earth.

WAR

It was a war so great and powerful and vicious
it almost gained consciousness;

it was so independent of any one part
we granted it citizenship in every country;

it was possessed of such a strong will
it was asked to attend a school for the gifted;

it fit perfectly enough into history
that we bought and sold it in galleries.

It ate our newborns, told bad jokes on stage,
crept up on scantily dressed women in alleys;

it cultivated the fat and the ugly in pens,
kept variety and beauty alive in a vat;

it changed the definition of *language*,
it let meaning die, then revived it with a shock;

it took the baby's breath out from behind
every rose and made bouquets of flesh and blood.

It was a war so quick and without origin that wine
lost its value and stopped aging in the cask;

it used politics and words to trick men
into giving up their spouses and lovers;

it held vandals accountable for poor penmanship
and made the rushed stand still as their buses left;

it brought father and son together to play
vengeance in the blood of children and the weak.

What happened in that moment of quick thought,
in the violence of an unconsidered action?

KITE

What are we teaching our children when
we caution against wax wings
yet give them kites that get tangled

in the overhead wires? A man's fingers shake,
belying the stillness he feels.
Is it some process, he wonders, some rushing

of blood to some unreachable destination,
functioning without his consent?
As much as he feels he's stopped, must he go on?

That sound of a kettle boiling is the sea,
that breaking of glass, the sky.
In the cries of newborns some of us

in tune with the future can already hear
whispers of death.
Who will keep us from our shame

by enfolding us within his own? Who will
name his skull Infamy, claiming
those who dwell within its ethereal walls?

Nobody said this was how it had to be,
but none spoke against it either.
What responsibility do we have to the road

ahead as opposed to that beneath our feet?
Who will act as scout,
that lonely occupation for which one

receives a parade at the outset
and is stoned on return?
How can we resist so rhythmic a tide

except by drowning? How can we resist
the wind if we rule out erosion?
The broken record still plays for half a revolution.

Nature, the philosopher says, *is engaged
in a hunger strike on our behalf.*
The stillness at the core of this moment

is identical to that which falls immediately
after an orator's last words:
the perfect instant when the last waves

of physical sound have flooded past
the last listener's ears;
the moment when those assembled have not

yet decided whether to burst into applause
or trample one another in panic,
each flapping limb tangling with the next,

the boughs of a tree being knotted by a hot wind.
Hell, he says, *is yet ravenous,
and it won't be full until you get there.*

Lion

Having found their buried road,
you have decided you know much

about the people who stopped travelling west:
there was a change of leadership,

a catastrophe, a shortage
of cobblestones or food, a terrible

disease among the men of working age,
a propaganda campaign

against people not of the East.
Take your teeth out if you must,

but keep your tongue in;
words will only aggravate a situation

that was degrading even before
you arrived with your flags and horse,

a thousand years late for war.
Another summer of scrub fires

is what kept this road from completion,
another shortage of funds,

another political filibuster.
Yes, that's it, another prowling lion

that terrorized the workers in the night,
another dire reading of the stars

by some half-baked oracle, another no,
                              another yes.

ANCHOR

Here he comes, this man whose approach
could kick up a dust cloud in a land of fens, this man
who flings himself into the lives of others

as though a shell shot from beyond
the horizon, this man of few words, but these. Perhaps
we should cut the world's flagpoles

in half and be done with it. The penitent have taken
to licking the floors and bedsheets
in leper colonies, to bathing last in the cold water

left after a long line of plague victims
have been washed for burial. The words *apathy*
and *sympathy* are claiming a relationship

to *pathology*. The planet is a pill in a pestle
and night is the shadow of the approaching
chemist. A ship of flour drops an anchor

of salt off a shore of sugar, the ocean
eroding all three quickly enough that before
the men can disembark they find themselves lost

at sea. Cream refuses to mix with coffee, apples
stay green and sour, leaves cling to the trees and die
without turning, fiddleheads fail to unfurl

into ferns and the loam of the forest floor is bathed
in sunlight. Pavement never cracks
and thousands of students go unemployed, pens

around the world simultaneously run dry
and ink pots tip, the sun stops directly overhead,
rendering sundials useless and stealing

from humanity the ability to check hairstyles
without the use of a mirror! Coincidentally, the foam
of ale that clings to the inside rim

of one young woman's pint glass relates,
in the original Arabic, the adventures
of Scheherezade's fifth cousin. In the distance,

a pulsar lets out one long burst that shows no sign
of subsiding; the planet's astrology community
is decimated. The elderly are disposed of

in landfills, tamped down into mine shafts
with heavy machinery. Legs and arms stick out
everywhere. Maybe the war-crimes tribunals

of the future will charge invaders
with littering. The juries should be comprised
of children to ensure

swift and remorseless death
for the convicted. Buried beneath the forest floor,
a protesting monk rings a bell over and over

as he meditates towards his death,
a surprising two weeks later. *The gods*, he says,
are drinking a tea boiled over the embers

of our homes and bones. The people
bearing witness in the jungle above
likely don't notice the final chime of his bell,

their ears carrying on the task of listening
long after he has fallen over cross-legged onto
his side. Yes, here he comes, and when

he finally arrives, this man will preach the dangers
of loving in an end-time, when events decide
the length and quality of bliss and retaliation

becomes the institution which governs
all relationships. In return for his wisdom
let us feed and bathe him and clothe him

in the trappings of a king, let us prepare
a great gallows from which he can be hung,
let us wait patiently for a rent to form in the earth,

into which he shall be thrown, our own anchor of flesh.

Steampipe

In the abandoned yard a steampipe
stands belching. The locals
have drawn markings in charcoal

around the lip and down the western side.
What still works below the fallow
soil? What mechanism goes unchecked?

Can it be a surprise in this remaining world
when any seemingly causeless system
produces an effect? Twenty miles away

a man who once played the flute by holding
its mouth to the pipe's flow of wet air
is taking his last sighs in the skin of some animal.

Two years ago he survived a bullet to the head
while hunting with a brother,
but is now dying of lead poisoning.

Somewhere below the very ground
on which my funerary wood is being erected,
he thinks, *that deep boiler huffs away,*

forgotten and long past its due.
Its emphysemic breath, mimicking the smoke
rising from the base of the pyre,

turns the gears in a machine
too big to be seen. What still feeds it? What fuel
propels its invisible inferno? *What a laugh,*

he thinks, slipping away
by the fire he watched his family build.
The rings of stone glow for long hours

after the embers blacken to charcoal.

Tenement

In the middle of this bus stop of a planet,
a desert's stretch of pavement

is the tongue of a dry god.
Everywhere her eye falls,

so too falls blood, and where her blood falls,
warrior children spring up

ready to both deny and continue existence.
People search the Vedas for answers,

investigate the teachings of the Buddha,
raid the words of God

in every language but come up with nothing
to justify all this anger.

The benches here have all tipped,
spilling their payload

of laziness to the concrete.
Sunset, our bride, our prophet's whore,

take no recompense in your station.
There on the edge of a heaven

the shepherd drives his flock of clouds.
Behind the billboards are the tenements,

behind the tenements, only sky.

Window

Close that time-frosted window with a stone,
close his mouth with your fist.
That dumb brute Samson was able to silence

the Philistines, why can't you? There comes
a point for all well-loved walls
when the number of hangings, past and present,

meet in an equation determining
structural integrity,
each nail biting into the wood boring out

its own little birth canal until the wall itself
resembles a senseless honeycomb
and the next nail has nowhere to go

but into the spackled cavern left
by one gone before. Here,
where attraction intersects with admiration,

here is where we spend our time
and call it love. Only now
after so many years have passed can we be sure

what the next season will bring. The gods
bathe in our flesh and we receive
and store their cast-away filth. Now,

come to think of it, this holds true
for well-hated walls as well:
each peephole, each suppurating bullet hole,

each angry fist. Sure, she cut his hair
but he was balding anyway.
It is hard to assign blame in situations

such as these.
                It's hard to tell the windows
from the stones, the eyes from the bullet holes.

Arrow

Significant glances are being exchanged
by insignificant people.
The consensus is: someone somewhere

is headed home. Archaeology's gift to us
has been a sense of self-importance;
the very walls around us have become film,

are capturing the images. Quick,
make a face:
we can't let the future think

we believed any of this! How absurd,
allowing our little lives
to be ruled by those retarded twins

prophecy and history. The bird
that makes its nest
in the rocks overlooking the sea

is the first to feel the slight tremors,
its hollow bones vibrating.
When it bolts into the blue above the surf,

a white bullet fired from the muzzle
of the planet itself,
it might regret leaving behind its eggs,

but safe in the shell of the sky, it will
never again have to feel the earth
tremble. We are running at a deficit,

operating at a loss. Even the milkweed
has gone off in the rays
of this unclean sun. Rocks

smoothed to egg shapes by the river
are hatching, chairs are being
made with only two legs at the front,

dumb cabbages out in the field
have taken over
the bearing and rearing

of our children. Those clouds in the distance
are picking up their pace.
Here is a secret: there is more weather

than anyone suspects. It flows
around us, thick and oily,
it moves in waves to soak us,

it is the perfect physical model
for time. A starving
and unskilled man waits on the beach

below the roost in the cliff-face,
his arrow drawn.
He predicts and fears his own failure

long before it has a chance
to confirm or deny
its being. In the surf swirling

around his feet are inedible fossils
of various, possibly extinct
species. He hails from a plentiful land

he hasn't seen in years; he lives off
what food he finds and kills
on roadsides. *What do we have*

to look forward to, he asks himself,
upon any return home?
Another contest to prove our identity

by bending a bow? His hungry arms are weak,
his elbows shake
as he struggles to keep his aim

and patience. *Allowed only one shot*
at a morsel whose meat
could mean life or death, not all of us

will make our mark, he thinks. *Yet everyone,*
given the muscular grip
gravity keeps on our bodies and missiles,

everyone is bound to hit something.

TIGER

Who set the wild on fire? Who cast the first
torch into the savannah's dry darkness

to light the world for hunting? Who raced
before the flames as though there was a chance

for survival under so borderless a sky? Who ran
into each city trailing the fire behind

as though a minor god of war? Who found
life as a messenger with tiny wings

of flame on the heel? Who flew the forest paths?
Who climbed the mountainside? Who cut

into the glacier followed by fire? Who arrived
at the edge of the jungle only to find

that even the wet planet can burn? Who ran
short of breath before the eager tongues

of flame? Who brought fire to the world
of the tiger? Who looked up at the array

of tiny lights in the sky as the red and black jaws
bore down snapping?

CELL

And the trains continue to run long after
the last passengers disembark:
the systems we built to self-execute

having executed us. The police blend
in with the pedestrians.
Somewhere one cop takes another down

in shackles and slams shut the door
of his cruiser. A pair
of boxer's sunglasses is your reward

for speaking up, an uncrossable
bridge of a nose;
when has tenderness ever been an issue?

The thieves who stole your sense
of well-being
are not beautiful enough

to know the danger of lust
let out of hand;
their savage Pistoia long since destroyed,

at least in memory. The men
who patrol this hot ring
do so with a macabre delight

in beating, burning, screwing metal
into the bones of our hands,
and yet you refuse to reveal yourself

and protect us with even a slender
word. Is there no way
to observe the mesh of gears that grinds

this clockwork universe into being
from any vantage other
than that offered from between the teeth?

These cells, neither castigatory
nor monastic, are boundless.
And the gaps between the bars offer only

the most frightening possibilities.

MARQUEE

Well, here we are: only late for the show
by moments or years, yet just in time

for the story to begin. And the marquee
that hangs over the empty square in the rain

is as black as the wall behind it. Though the glass
remains, there's not a single bulb

with filament intact. Yet by the buzz
in the mist one might suspect power still flows

through some of the copper wiring:
the intermittent current of marching ants

that once lit up the night and signalled the start
of something big, something beyond the everyday,

something to escape to: this. Just outside
the city limits the fish have returned to a lake

once so polluted even the weeds died. In fact,
the water is bountiful enough it looks as though

one might simply reach in and close
a fist around any flash of silver and come away

with a catch. All escape routes guarded
by their own bodies, the odds

of survival are better now than in the lottery
of an earlier time. This is

a species at its most raw: throwing itself
against the locked door of population

and starvation as though, given a proper pounding,
the hinges might fly off to reveal what lies

beyond. There is a pulse somewhere in the wet
darkness surrounding the theatre, a spark

that builds upon itself in a pleasurable world
of reverse physics. But of course an electric hum

could come from almost anything in these parts,
these days; and the show ended long ago

to bad reviews and an empty house. Looking out
from within a darkened room, you see a figure

standing in the open door and, when the door frame
empties suddenly, ask whether someone has

stepped into the room or out. Of course the only
sure way to tell what's going on beneath

the surface of water and glass is to remove
one of the black bulbs and slip a willing finger in.

ROAD

At the end of organized stones,
the dry earth takes up:

an infinitely wide road running
in all directions at once.

In the distance there hovers a sound
on the wind, some great machinery

clacking the dusk away.
Is it an apparatus of war? A giant loom?

An engine devoted to solving riddles?
One could be frightened

by such a sound, thinks the man
who stands at the end of the road.

It is faceless and directionless,
it has no sense of good taste or order.

I wonder, he thinks, stepping out
into the dust, *does it emanate*

from just below where the sun sets,
or just above, there in the black,

where the North Star quietly rises?

Diary

Stand outside this inner theatre and wait.
In one woman life develops a stutter
while from another the children fall cursing.

Who knows what negotiations take place
between a sudden urge
to create and a few moments of blood?

At some point in the evening the grass collects
its dew. The temperature drops
and air rolls from its restless sleep into water.

Is there a dewpoint of reason? Emotion?
Spirit? What happens when doubt
stretches out as though in a waking yawn

and finds its horizons the uterine walls
in which it is now kept
for its own and everyone else's safety?

Is it worth hoping there is a divine parent
waiting on a porch somewhere,
tortured by our every decision, praying

that all this living is but a passing phase?
The unborn try to speak
the way one perceives sound in a dream,

words understood without ever being

heard. It would be much less dark
in the night were all this earth not in the way.

A diary of worry is not needed. No other
explanation could better serve
the purpose we have brought with us.

SUGAR

No morning so hectic it is without time for us
to be born, no evening so booked we cannot find

a way to die. Collect what is dear to you
and keep it close; this is a world without chances

for second thoughts. Yes there's been melody
and yes there's been threnody

and yes both comedy and tragedy have existed:
but are we sugar? Will we melt in the rain,

whether it falls sweet on a summer's afternoon
or cold on an autumn eve? Will the rain

make us syrup? What about *this* rain,
hasn't it fallen on others? Where are

their bodies? Let us find proof!
In such a situation, it is not uncommon to feel

as though you might sit quietly forever,
forgetting to exist. In such a situation,

it's also not unusual to smile a moment
and remember that you've made it here,

so improbably, living in prehistory and aftermath,
Primavera and winter of discontent.

FIELD

The sky has been aged, is ancient enough now
to have lost its teeth, clamping one smooth gum

down on the other in a wry horizon's bite.
That the violence we have witnessed

was not random while the kindness was,
how insulting to our attempts at existentialism!

Can we not even frighten ourselves
with philosophy any more? That intent

could replace randomness as our greatest fear
speaks of how far we've come;

from there to here, from right to just left of right,
from fallen to the lower part of down. The corn

that stretches into the distance,
once an orderly army, has grown slack, wild,

and hoary, each stalk standing at ease
instead of attention, and in a place of its choosing,

bearing those heavy yellow arms in a silence
similar to hushed anticipation. Listen to the wind,

the brewing rain, the field, the flight
of distant machinery, the coded plan of attack.

Train

The spider at the centre of its web catches embers
floating up from the fire, sucks the life from them,

retreats to its schematic heart. Shy away, stay safe,

keep back from those nuns: who knows
where they've been? The hot hands of the young

stray deeper into diminishing fabric. Archipelagos

stretch away, a series of moments remembered,
peaking from the wet of life. Dream,

the longest dramatic performance in history,

continues despite all efforts to the contrary. The stars
reflect a constellation in the mirror. O light,

to have travelled so far and be forced to turn back,

now when there's something to fall on! The people
hereabouts could not find their way to heaven

were they tied bodily to a priest. The rain

carries a permanence it lacked in its youth,
a resolve; some might call it a maturity. Outside

people speak of infidelity, the moon waxes,

sweat pours from the spouts on our necks. The heart
of the embryo races, a tiny genetic train.

Cage

A period of least resistance is upon us. Quickly,
finish everything! Only nothing
may be left undone. Do you now find it

impossible to look strangers in the eye
without speculating where
the surgeon's pen might mark their forehead

with the crosshairs of future incisions?
In an infinite number of books
written by one monkey at one typewriter

where only one key still works, it states that
someday some intrepid explorer
will follow the overhead ducts to their source,

and the darkness that sweeps the edges
of our understanding
will be mapped. The wall around

this garden is a metaphysical one,
an insurmountable idea
that keeps us out and heaven in. Assuming

our bodies will be left where they fall,
which do you bet
will eat us first, the birds or the worms?

Will the worms eat us and in turn
be eaten by birds? Will we climb
the food chain from the inside? Will we rise

as though a gorge, as though a hand reaching up
from the depths of the lion's throat?
Are these questions pointless, or are they

points without question? Hell-on-earth
has been in the planning since
shortly after Heaven-on-earth was abandoned.

Maybe all this worry can be cured,
perhaps we are suffering
without need, maybe the answers we wish

would find us already have, are resting
on the backs of our tongues,
waiting for a cool drink of water. There is

a difference between a prison and a cage,
though such subtleties are lost
on some. We are now tied together, friend,

in modes more unfortunate than blood.

PIKE

Enjoy these light-headed moments
because eventually your
eyes will feel as heavy as stones.

Each half-year is only a nickel
of the decade:
would that we were richer still, or more miserly.

We are sailing these unknown seas
in a medicine bottle;
we are steering with a slender pestle.

Look out there on the street: our children
run amok, playing ball
with the helmets of our soldiers,

pouring water and goldfish
into the airtight bowls
favoured by our astronauts.

The city's buildings are thick incense sticks
against the cobalt sky
and the wind is blowing the scent

of their burning across the countryside.
The only way to digest this
is to mimic the birds and swallow

enough broken stones to help.
Is the pike all this news
comes down a pointed pole

on which rests the head of a rebel leader,
or just another kind of fish?
Begin, O cosmic weavers, to spin your loom

and make for us tuques and flannel!
The weathermen say
it's going to be a hell of a winter

and there are still so many repairs
to reckon with.
The bellies of our men are barely covered.

Try to look on the mystery of life
as a playing card might:
it is natural to be shuffled and dealt.

We may still be resting and playing today
but tomorrow is Monday,
and on Monday everyone has to work.

Only at the maddest party is the talk
of retribution
and only at a funeral does no one speak.

If the old texts are right and nothing
but a column
of smoke holds up the heavens,

then we must all work together
to keep the fires burning
so Paradise might never fall to earth

and we might never be crushed
                              under bliss.

EMBLEM

Listen: the mantis on the flower opens
her mandibles and waits, a frozen war emblem.

There was barely time to touch the surface
with a stone awl, much less scratch a name.

The games these Masons play: burying jars of milk
by the river against some war too secret to tell.

Speak: everything opined of the end
will be true, if only in that moment's outcome.

When seen moving through the dust motes
and the rotating fan's flickering shadow,

even the grass leaves muddy tracks, breaking camp
and marching an endless, singing army out to combat.

STATUE

Suddenly the statuary is upon us,
hovering with panicked airs.
Why didn't we notice it sneaking up?

Guilt has unexpectedly become tangible,
is falling from its bearers
in tears of marble and limestone;

shall we rebuild the cracked white pillars,
the chipped plinths?
Shall we quarry here in the light

and air above ground? Free
of the weight of fault,
might we finally shoot into the sky

as we were obviously destined to?
Or, without ballast,
will we tip at the crest of the next wave?

What is the danger of speaking
against this in one's head?
That someone might be listening?

It was a good but rocky world
as recently as yesterday.
It is there to see in all the papers of record,

in all the shadows painted on the walls
of our caves. What was bound
to happen? This. Despite how unlikely

the events of our fall may seem,
there was always
a hundred per cent chance

things would turn out this way. Prophecy,
it seems, is almost always just
an unrestrained case of history envy.

(Painfully the mountains sing of emptiness;
grudgingly the oceans
                     do not.)

STAIRCASE

There is a conspiracy among siblings to look alike;
there is a stain waiting to mar a perfect white blouse.

That the rabbit hole with so small an opening

might widen on the other side: now that's trust.
Fibonacci's skull held to the light casts

kaleidoscope shadows on the floor.

Accident/coincidence/pattern; the aphids
are holding mirrors up to our mouths.

A spiral so perfect one weeps to see it;

where did that damn staircase go?
The wondrous thing about falling is the moment

of release from the expectations of a certain gravity.

BED

So, what, now the tired are finally waking?
A queue has formed at the Siege Perilous.
The sleepers are slipping deeper into that unlit self.

Sir Dagonet, only you can save us now!
Bearing a torch into darkness is noble indeed.
When Tiamat comes seeking Babylon, someone point.

Our minds are all meat in the same soup.
Gautama, I wasn't listening: what did you say just now?
Our inheritance has finally stood us up.

So much flying white it looks like flying black.
At least now we can say we know nothing's coming.
Only the murkiest salamanders will not sweat.

Eternity is taking for-fucking-ever to get here.
Only the fire-eaters and the carousels will be spared.
Anger is the floral-patterned upholstery of emotion.

Solomon to Sheba: *Just who do you think you are?*
History is a bowl, ma Cherry, terse and sweet.
Unwrap the gold foil and find, what? Another damn coin?

Have you tried lately to unforget something?
Hungry orphans are so easy to fool.
We could stay young forever simply by moving West.

Cleopatra sideways in a mirror, sucking in her gut.
Wisdom: when the sun sinks, it's time for bed.
Should a fly buzz, close the covers with a snap.

Trap

It's getting harder to recognize one another
in these disguises of flesh;

the mothers of the world are short of breasts,
having given up bearing children to drop litters.

If the sky is truly the blue skin of Kali,
then we are being crushed inside her fist.

Lay down your weapons and cross the field:
we are entering a time

when one battalion should welcome
the next with open arms.

It is time to begin discussing the terms
of your surrender, starting with the forfeiture

of everything you hold dear
and the abandonment of your beliefs.

The people of your nation are sore
in the bones, but there is no room here

in which to stretch, much less to give others
a gentle rub on the small of the back.

Life, our best thinkers say, is a string
of pearly beads given in trade for peace,

for a stretch of identity and the chance
to be next to one another a brief moment.

The random shape our flesh takes
is that of the mould of reality

into which we were long ago poured:
the undeniable pressure

of the earth, air, water,
the everything in which

we solidify shaping us
as surely as any sculptor's hand.

So while we are, let us embrace in public spaces,
let us couple with strangers in the street,

let us seek out others with an intimate eye
and recognize their thought with love.

In the shade of an olive an unseen child
gnaws on a grisly shank of meat,

much as a coyote in a trap might eschew
her leg in favour of further opportunity.

Release your hand from the form
of a weapon, hold it to your ear:

that sound you hear isn't the rain
that has been sent to cool the burnt earth.

It's a strand of beads that has been cut
in the middle of its catenary curve;

it's the sound of pearls dropping two by two,
trickling down the hanging helix of bare chain.

Desert

Even here (so far from anywhere it almost can't be
called here) someone has laid milestones:
a countryless border stretching into the desert,

the first measuring fingers of society. The obsession
with place and distance preceding and succeeding men
by leagues and years; a land so free of the concept

of confinement it has yet to encounter the basic idea
of space. Here a shiver could run through
a man as though it were the last of his soul:

a single seed rattling in the dried gourd
of his skin, a drop of water in a cured deer's bladder
carried on the hip, a sigh in the mouth

at the moment of last breath. Here the spirit is either
dwarfed by the body, lying fetal and quiet
as the head of an unstrung fiddle, or it grows

inconceivably bold, pushing against the flesh: a bird
smashing itself on the bars of a cage, a dog spitting
and choking at the end of a chain, a baby

lying stunned in torn clothes. Yes, here the spirit
is a child: impatient to get naked and free,
eager to see what's out there, to see what's offered

by the measure of space it can occupy.

Plane

The plane in the hangar might still attempt flight
in whatever dreams machines can muster.

Money is irrelevant: belief means enough
of the same item in one place constitutes a bank.

Set against the desert, the lead rain
and the glass lightning seem a strange pair.

By which metre is this ship's progress rowed?
On what drum is the foreman's order beaten?

(this has been such a sandy pit
                              from which to scramble)

When they need it, today's aircraft just clear
some sky, the aviator's equivalent of icebreaking.

Please clarify: is that pattern in the dry steppe
meant to be a landing pad or a target?

HOURGLASS

In the torso of the woman's dress the spines of a corset
can be seen, if one looks close enough at the photo:

a Promethean armour, an extended rib cage
protecting her liver, spleen, and other punishable

organs from the beaks of birds. Think of the amount
of sand required to make a single shapely hourglass.

In the desert there is a gathering of craftsmen
that make glass for the manufacture of timepieces.

It is the black remains of crushed cities, they say,
that best allows the grains to slide

from one globe to the next and in turn tells time
most accurately. Somewhere, buried in the dirt

of the desert, is a picture of a man in an ill-fitting
wedding suit: his shoulders slender, his neck

so thin it rises at an angle from the collar,
the post and clapper of a bell. It looks as though

if you shook him hard enough he might ring. *Stock up,*
says an old man, gesturing expansively toward

the horizon where the sun sits, a pot of sand boiling
over a fire lit on a kindling of archaeological treasure.

We are just this close to running out.

STORM

The river holds many secrets, not the least
of which is the horizon: on one side
a jagged cityscape, on the other only a hill

and trees. Huddled on one bank a man waits out
the storm to gather information about fate:
where will the lightning that drops upon his life

fall? Where will its marks be seen in the earth
of his skin? He has questioned before:
is he the shore or the wave that breaks against it?

Is he the earth or the river? Is he the blue or the bolt
that hurtles from it? Hunting in the deep of a wood,
will it be the last cobble of a long-dead society

on which he steps and cripples himself?
This portentous thunder sets off
the alarms of the future, sets the prophets

to mumbling, sets the illustrated deck of cards
near the window sill to whirling,
sets the world's pregnant women to labour,

their fruit being spilled in a forced autumn
with no uniformity of ripeness.
Why does the fading storm, moving into

the distance, not trigger the same apprehension
as the one approaching? What some
might call hope, others call folly. *Wild accusations*

require villains to be taken seriously,
so if you are going to create one, he thinks, *consider*
creating both. A tame flock of white doves

has been groomed and trained to return
to the cage so they may be released
time and again at special events;

we have constructed ourselves as creatures
of forgetfulness to accommodate structures
such as these. Mercy is on ration,

goodwill in short supply:
if we hoard, we may survive, or perhaps
our preserves will spoil in their limestone jars.

Stand facing a wall that rises to just above eye level,
look at the strip of sky that kisses its lip,
ask yourself whether this line of blue represents

the horizon. Do the arms of your fellow man
hold an embrace or a strangling yoke?
Who set the fathers of the world to weeping?

Who can make them cease? What thunder
truly breaks that does not bring
with its flash any man's momentary fright?

Ask yourself, is there a person alive for whom
the rending of the air holds no significance?
In this regard are we not all prophets?

Much as we have recently realized

that the river continues to, at the very least,
somewhere around the bend,

is not the knowledge of our own frailty
also a version of mass prophecy,
a telling of the future momentarily upon us?

Bear

Shall we treat the serpents to blood from our necks?
Shall we open our skulls so the monkeys might feast?

Shall we pick the fruit of our eyes and feed them

to one another as though they were cored sour apples?
These models we've made of the universe

turn it to stone, create the equivalent of a stuffed bear

rising in the corner of a gentleman hunter's study,
ferocious and snarling for all time, yet utterly powerless

to frighten those who believe it to be dead.

When the crest broke from that last wave, the world trembled;
that keystone shard could be what keeps reality's

arch from crumbling around us; could be the one spine
of hull that would bear the essential weight of sea.

The black dogs of invention bed down in the moors;
the robe and crown hang in a closet without light.

Masked on either side of and/or and/or and/or;
what happens where intellect and emotion meet?

Each fissured brain with workings complex as a pill;
the catenary's curve is all that keeps us straight.

The bear traps lie open, the mouths of buried children;
the neat earth is quiet and groomed, pregnant with mines.

Turn back the clocks an hour every night for a year;
roll back the stones only from the graves of your friends.

Now: we're sinking; O god, think, remember: that splint
er of wave: where last did you see it; and/or: who has it?

FLAG

It makes more sense now to use
the white flag we've been saving as a tourniquet,
and when we peel it

from the empty arteries of the dead
its mottled stains will sign a next, lonely nation.
Sing to the new children:

O children leaping from our heads,
O birth without pain, O minds emptied quick
as tipped urns!

Might we touch one another and be
revealed? In the murky dark between rooms
the business of inheritance continues.

Hold your tongue, my hands seem to be full.

CROWN

Overhead it looks like the cranes
might be returning,
though there are pessimists among us

who will tell you they are just leaving
somewhere else. The planet
has recently ascended to a new dimensional

altitude and billions of ears
have just popped,
which is (in and of itself) nothing new,

but on an empty globe any sound can be
deafening. Left of here,
there was once a doctor who specialized

in the reattachment of conjoined twins
for whom individuality
just wasn't working out. He used to tell

the story of seeing a man who tried to fashion
a crown of loose sand,
who kept refilling the cup of his hands

from the desert floor and trying to cover
his brow with a dirty coronet.
The power fell away through the holes

between his fingers, slipping down as though
simply ill-fitting from his temples
and into his eyes. While very much a man

of peace he knew those who weren't
and even sometimes
counted them among his friends. *Tolerance,*

he would say, *is always the wrong word,*
but so is acceptance.
This from a man who tried to walk on water

but came away with leeches on the soles
of his feet. Yes, it's true:
someone too smart for our own good once

weighed the universe and found it too heavy
for what could be seen, creating
a mild curiosity about our control over

consumption. It all began with an open mouth
and the desire to fill it;
it will end with femurs used as knitting needles

and enormous skeins of intestinal wool.
Or so say our best prophets.
The same men who, with their eyes

blinded by the blowing sand and ash,
see the cranes with their
lightning-bolt necks and peaked crowns

returning to our skies in mating pairs
yet can only mark the sadness
of withdrawal in other, less-ravaged lands.

Minefield

Brush holly on this mess, brush oak,
treat the land with a poultice
of holy water and wort,

heal the holes in the ground with salves
made of moss and earth.
Use fireweed, use morphine, use hemlock,

stuff the craters with dark soil
and the seeds of wildflowers.
Replace Your Divots! the sign reads

at the mouth of the minefield.
One day we will decorate
with beehives and razor blades.

One day we will coat the walls
with various combinations of excreta.
One day water will refuse to blast

from the mouths of canons
and protestors will run wild,
and the buildings so calculatingly cleaned

of nuclear shadows will accumulate
the bacchanal silhouettes of a riot.
The helmet on this head is a pea,

has stopped a bullet,
but the head rests on a spike
instead of a neck!

Dear Lord, they removed the chain
from his tongue and replaced it
with a ball of surgical steel.

He now speaks twice as often,
but only half as well. Each gulf, each pit,
each cavity and its accompanying stain,

each ghostly limb of a passerby,
those partial absences, beg us to question
whether there will ever be another Rome,

another Sumer, Xanadu, Bethlehem.
Whether there has ever been
a presence with our best interests in mind.

WOLF

The architect of the cottage on the hill
never took into account
its foundations. Having been paid

for a hasty erection, he forgot what damage
the ages might do
to a dwelling built in a passion for ease.

It's not the noise of the city that distracts,
it's the narrative.
It's the urge to pluck order, a through-line,

purpose, from the seeming chaos. It's the need
to make sense from nonsense
that occupies waking moments and coaxes

inactivity from accomplishment.
O for a pair of red eyes
in the woods. What should we fear

in an age that has killed emergency,
when stakes of destruction
have been jacked so high no one

can match the ante? The kindness
in the eyes of the dog
is not the opposite of the malice

dripping from the wolf's maw. For now
we must share these shadows
with the dark, for it does not have its own.

For now we must go where they
do not want us.
For now we must explore.

BOOK

A tattered storybook found in the dirt
relates the tale of an awful ogre

who ate his employer because the six-figure
salary he received was one girl short

of what he requested. *There once was
a six-armed goddess,* another begins,

*who still felt she needed an extra hand
around the house . . .*

In the middle of the last story, a man
we all know is described in embarrassing detail:

he worked all his life to get himself
a trophy wife only to realize years later

she was for third place. Also in the dust
is a survival manual that, when opened,

only repeats the word *Run!* over and over
and over. Beside each book is another,

and another: a graveyard of philosophy,
mathematics, fairy tale, physics,

ethics, science fiction, sociology, language.
Do you think Fate, one heavier tome asks,

stepped back from her work one day
and was surprised to find a pair of blue jeans

on the loom? From this distance
it's hard to tell whether she was the kind

of craftsman whose concentration rests
at the needle or on the swatch of fabric

stretching into the distance.
If you want to broaden your horizons,

says the volume on Zen, *go live on a hill.*
Sleep is a form of time travel. The soul

works like a yo-yo. Heaven and Hell
both last only an instant, but death is the end

of our ability to perceive time.
Everyone remain calm!

There is one useful bit
not found in any text on the ground:

the sails of those six ships on the horizon
have had the centres cut from them.

Even with a good wind,
they can't land anywhere near here soon.

There is no need for all this panic, all this hope.

Bomb

The elderly mind is a fuse burning
back to an implosion of birth, but age
cannot touch the core of identity.

While life is still moving in the fast lane,
the road has turned to gravel. The body
is a tool that allows us to put faces

to whatever souls we might already know;
recognition is a gift that separates
us from each molecule of water.

Once again the world has been turned over
on itself: soil prepared for seeding.
It seems a more talented gravedigger

might have used his shovel to cut us holes
in the sky, might bury us six feet up,
well on our way to Heaven. The spirit

we all so desperately seek to define
departs the body in a panic:
fleeing as though there is only one

emergency exit in the theatre,
as though an old lover just called
to say she's naked and waiting, as though

having forgotten a child in public.
Which is it the cinema advises
its bomb-squad officers to cut first, the red

wire or the blue? When the fuse runs out,
memory goes forever,
leaves as though abruptly hit

with the realization that there are
more important things to do.
Can't we help but fiddle with the wires

and keep from dying of curiosity?
O what mysterious
seduction goes on with abandon?

Carving

In the long line of refugees moving between borders,
a child tugs at his mother's hem, asks whether
the time before birth is the same as death. In a lesson

from years before, the mother remembers asking
a prophet whether the world's broken statues
bled, whether they spilled organs and red rope

as they were toppled. Out on the lake, the ducks
slowly sink to their shoulders, yet still paddle
their periscope necks about as though nothing

out of the ordinary has happened. Nearby, an artisan
uses a blade to shape wood and thinks
that it is perhaps not unlike the knife some god

might have used to shape him or may still use
to take his life away. Genealogies
will never be the same, nor will caravans. *Let us*

learn to exist, he thinks, *without trust*
in the concept of usual. How disconcerting is it
to meet your best friend's twin

and realize you've known the evil one all your life?
At what point does wreckage become rubble
before slowly sliding through time to ruin?

Shadow has the physical properties of water when
pooled in a skull exposed to the evening's slanted light.
Deep in a hole in the earth, a mining pony

stares mutely at the caged bird that no longer sings
as the men continue to sting the stone
with spades and picks, effectual as a scorpion

against the sole of a good boot. In the distance
a church bell swings high in its tower,
but with the sides worn through by years of use

the clapper strikes nothing but air and silence rings
out, the second thought of an explosion
that occurred moments before. No wonder then

the refugees are deaf and cross-eyed. The river
isn't without the mirror quality of the still
lake's surface. In fact it is exactly the same,

only with thousands of surfaces in a finger's breadth,
millions, each reflecting with absolute clarity
whatever image it faces at the moment of its advent

and ruin. The world is filled with the scent
of soil turned up by the passing of hooves and feet,
telling of a recent exodus in one direction

or another. One stroke too many of the chisel
and the distracted artisan has penetrated
the final sliver of wood, spoiling a work he wished

only to be delicate. Later, a man on the horizon kneels
over the discarded carving, his head bowed
against the powerful ball of sun. He is struggling

to catch up with a procession that passed this way
thousands of years before. He is trying
to recover his breath after realizing history

is not only the prey he hunts, but the beast
he suspects has been tracking him from behind.

Harbour

On either side of awe stand horror and reverence.
The lawyer knows: it is language that erodes
memory. Keep that witness silent unless you intend

him to testify. From the callused knees of the pious
to the muddy feet of the fisherman, blood flows
with the viscous speed of liquid helium: slipping away

from its massive edge and centre both at once,
a furious effort to cast a frictionless net over the feral.
Surely our Einsteins considered the curve of acceptance,

the likelihood of any one generation's missing
the opus of the last, or maybe the next?
Dozing in the lee of a cliff is now considered

consent regarding the layer of shale in which
your fossil will form; simply walking the earth
in silence is deemed a binding contract. One day

someone will mine that tier of oil, that stratum
of coal, that violent deposit, now hung
in the earth's memory, that was once you.

Approach the sun on your knees even as it stalks away.
Counsel, approach the bench, nice and slow:
remind the judge and jurors what words might compel

understanding. Our blood trawls faith's delta, a lattice

of cells seeking a hold from which to brave
the pushing of time's river out into the deep of the harbour.

Surely our Ptolemys had some starry rationale
for how to tack away from a harvest
of tongues in the current of a retrograde wave.

BRIDGE

In the mist it appears as though the metal bridge
spans the distance between left and right,
between nowhere and there:

on one end it disappears into a cloudy hill,
on the other it arrives at, or leaves from,
a vague group of buildings.

Any pilgrim who appears out of the thick air
on one side disappears to the other.
Even a bystander can hear

the elderly workman lost in the fog at the base,
his hammer echoing in the wet air.
The maul has been worn

down to a nub, the saw's edge is toothless
and monofilament-thin, only strokes
from non-existence.

On the hill the trees spit down their leaves insolently,
as they have a million times before, but this time
the insult seems serious.

Here all travellers advance as sleepwalkers might,
eyes wide and blind but for an arm's reach
on either side; the air is thick enough

that each pace is a leap of faith, a devotee's step

forward without assurance that the next
will yield purchase.

In the mind of every person lost on this bridge,
there is a space where another coming out
of the mist on the back of a mule

is a celebrity: bearing the fame of the land ahead,
a presence that guarantees somewhere to land,
as well as a vindication of trust.

What will become of the road when all who
understand the importance of mobility
have moved on?

Will it be the craftsman who outlasts the tools
or the last tool that outlasts
the craftsman?

The bell of the hammer on metal will cease
sooner than any suspects and the bridge
will eventually groan away,

evaporating into the mist, leaving the sandals
of would-be travellers exposed to whatever
water or soil or fire rushes below.

That a crossing has been made at any time
since the metal went up is a miracle;
that it has been done so

over and again is unthinkable.

CAMEL

Sing out your metred prayers as though
each god were deaf in one ear:
tilt yourself towards one pole or another

in an effort to speak. The straw that broke
this camel's back
was the first to be laid

and every piece since has been its burial.
Are the spices and incense
carried across a desert so hot it cooks

the mind worth more than those
brought by sea?
At the first blush of flame, the sudden rise

in colour, the earth seems embarrassed,
feverish, livid. In a world
of new medicines one must be careful

not to mistake flowers spent of petals
for simple weeds. Just as
the perfume trapped in the candle

needs fire to release it, so too must the cry
bide its time in the throat.
No one wants to write songs about

what's missing, but who wants to sing

about what's here?
Surely, anything is possible.

But then again,
                    the vast majority of anything
is highly unlikely.

HELM

O angelic sailors, cast anchor in our flesh.
O gods, ride your quiet cutters through our species.

Ignore the seamen that retch near the rail: each tear
an anchor to which someone forgot to tie a chain.

O awe! Our sails grow, inseminated with breath;
we all slide forward, captives to the helm and wind.

Sign

In a season of hardship one might eat anything:
no stalk or leaf too bitter, no lick
of flesh between ribs trivial enough to be ignored.

The fires in the distance are so hot they scorch
the birds from the sky;
the people whose horizon touches

this scene are upset only at the distance between
them and the cooked meat. A hot wind
rushes by, eager to nourish the destruction.

It whips the hair of every villager it passes,
fills the sail of every warboat,
imbues as though with a soul every flag

and mariner's semaphore. A man approaches
cautiously in an iron crown,
stands a silhouette in the door, his hands

held before him in a gesture of peace,
psalms up. He is a man with
a chequered past, it is said, but all the squares

are white. *Heaven*, he tells us, *is re-evaluating
its stance on good and evil,
and quite likely a population change*

will follow. He is hungry, polite, and will work
for food; he is well-read
and tells the stories of his people with flair.

The prey he was tracking by its blood-litter
has escaped him
(the long ropes of its intestines stretched

into red velvet barriers that seem to say
you may not pass this point
ceasing suddenly outside the village).

He sees no point in going on.
Some miles back, he says,
there stood on the roadside a sign

that read Bump Ahead, *and since then*
the entire human race
has sat hunched over the wheel,

apprehensively watching the landscape slip by
below, forever smooth and yielding.
In the glow of two fires (one for cooking

the day's kill and one approaching on the plain)
the king takes a breath,
collects his twin shadows,

and flees into the lee of the light.
The winds of change
that follow him kick up a corpuscular

dust into the eyes of the gathered.
Is it the very dirt from which
we were created that stings us into blindness

and tears, he asks, *or is it the bleary remnants*
of that long sleep before life
which we still have yet to rub away?

Harp

When the North Star rests just above the horizon,
the night spins past his eyes
and all he sees is the blade of a circular saw

cutting into the wood of the earth.
Thus we are separated
from men, he thinks. *I cannot hold two thoughts*

together, cannot wake the connections
between them;
I am only conscious of every third, fifth, seventh,

eleventh epiphany, those moments in between
staying between, paths
grown over. When he looks again

and the helm of night steers past his gaze,
the North Star
directly above, he asks:

Have I moved? Am I now on the horizon?
Is this how it works,
that one might travel from beginning

to destination and forget most of the road between?
He thinks, *Perhaps*
these reflections that seem so stranded

are paths themselves, the missing connections
simply the shadowy woods
that frame them. When the first heavy eyelids

of sleep begin to claim him, the stars
in all directions
blur into an iron wheel,

the cross-section of a harp string;
each fiery ball
in the distance the pluck of one taut note.

(The roof of his mouth throbs, just once, but heavy,
as though all the blood
is fleeing his body in favour of the brain.)

Siege

In the dark outside the city, a lone man
stands and declares a siege,

his voice ringing out but drowned
by the traffic only feet from his body.

He says the fur coat he wears
is made of the balding pates of accountants

and bureaucrats. He is angry
that we are always skipping the middles,

leaping from stone to stone over a brook
that might well have only come

to our ankles anyway. *Honey!* he shouts.
The trees run with it, the flowers

are fountains of it! It is a different world
now, one where bunches of grapes

can grow from our bellies,
where the valleys of our navels

should roll rich with orchards,
where our armpits could be jungles

ripe with unknown medicines. Bullets
should be bouncing off everything

in days such as these. The lock is divorced
from the door, the wing has left

the plane, the rooster has always
had a taste for chicken, every raindrop

is the miscarriage of a storm! Nothing
can be taken for granted, he cries,

until the moment we transcend ourselves!
I hold this to be self-evident.

His voice grows hoarse and fades in the night
and in the morning the last thing

anyone hears him asking is
if every crack in the walk

is the boundary of a chessboard square,
what are the chances we are each

any given piece? Days later, when his voice
is gone and the lip-readers are brought in,

they can unanimously agree on only one thing:
he's trying to tell us something.

Look! Out there! they think he's saying.
Our children are dancing

       to the tapping canes of the blind!

DYKE

The city has metastasized. The couriers weave
between chariot and hovercraft,
satchels filled with email written on papyrus.

Eyes grow from potatoes, moles from our skin:
useless limbs that somehow still leave
a ghostly itch when amputated. The child

we raised in a box has been lost in the mail.
All rulers want only
yes-men and mutes by their side.

Before lies are spoken can they be considered
mere experiments in the truth?
Do the buffalo know they graze on the edge

of evolution, straddling what line exists
between the ox in its yoke
and the winged bulls of Nineveh?

The water has risen and though we built
a million more dykes,
each has sprung an erotic leak.

Dutch Boys of the world UNITE!
Our hour is upon us!
The most supple among us can take eleven,

the rest must be content with being a hero
to but one. How glorious
is it to be held hostage no longer by

the longest shadows between the trees?
Would you not take
an unknown yet predictable goblin over this?

Close your eyes against the dark.
Listen to the wheels
spinning on the wet streets:

the mail goes round in circles but never seems
to find its way back here.
Questioning need not always be pained

with answering. Look down: your patience
is water held in the hands
and your fingers are beginning to ache.

Albatross

In what ways are we responsible for one another
as kin? In what ways are we free? Dear Lord,
could any of our worst fears have been imagined?

What did you think we'd use this awful sense for?
Somewhere over the ocean a rigid albatross
that hasn't moved in months rides dead in the clouds,

buoyed and kept aloft by coincidence of the wind.
Let us itemize each other's duties and present them
in clear plastic bindings. Let us stage

hand-puppet shows, create charts and graphs
so the idiotic and managerial among us might
finally understand. Let us write gibberish

and surrender it to the control-freak intellectuals
to edit and puzzle over. Send out your winged
messengers with nothing but screams

in their scroll cases, break out your leadless pencils,
your invisible ink that only works in the dark.
                              What else is there

to relate
                    but this:

FOREST

Seconds after it takes root in the tinder mix
of scrub and new brush,
your fire releases a breath of smoke

that lifts up as though it is an elderly man
rising from an age-old crouch.
What you found in the woods near the lake

so suits your needs:
a tree in which to store your goods, a brook
with clear water to wash wounds, fresh grass,

an overhung knoll in which to sleep.
You have been busy with the life
of a hunter:

the watching, the gathering, the stalking,
killing, carving, the emptying of meat
from skin, the removal of heads.

A thought shoots across the red and blue
mist of your mind,
mimicking a star streaking across

the banded twilight;
a particular omen in the length of its tail.
There will pass in childbirth a woman,

you've seen the vision:
the grey water of the drowned falling from
her mouth, running down her neck and breasts

as though she is the source of a spring.
On the lake where the moon has turned
the water to milk,

a lone man in a canoe drifts by
and you cannot tell whether
he is looking at you or the dying fire

or the dark ring of the forest. *Nothing will
ever be perfect again,* you
think, falling back into sleep;

your encampment's bed will forever
be made with sheets of stone,
the love made under the damp covers

breeding only darkness and cold silence.

SUNDIAL

In the few moments we have under the sky
we are but time, walking.
Look out from the gnomon of your heels.

Turn, run, gallop, make what moment you need
by keeping ahead of the dusk.
Pluck everything you want from the space

between your shadow and where the sun
warms the molten soil.
We have constructed the division

of age into all the wrong units:
it has been the same day
since you were born, the same hour,

the same minute. Your shadow is trying
to tell you something.
Turn sideways: see its lips moving?

The sundial fence posts that stretch away
in long lines have no such
advantage. Perhaps somewhere the sun casts

its own shadow against something akin
to numerals hewn in the earth.
What it sees its mouth say might be

almost unpronounceable with our tongues,
but is not inconceivable.

BULL

You don't have to be Minoan to know the desire
to leap this bull. Knossos, O Knossos!

Have your lithe soldiers sharpen their axes
and meet us on the field of tomorrow.

The strippers shed layer after layer yet can't seem
to get naked enough. Soon it will be only

the skeleton we find erotic. The inevitable is
all the things you plan to do when thinking of death

meeting guiltily in your mind with everything
you've done. Think of the difference between

the fisherman and the swimmer. Think of the moments
of peace between each bullet, between each breath.

What chance could there be that this one question,
this very considered action, might make it through to you,

so far in the distances of time? Can you hear me?

REEF

Cooling, the earth is still cooling.
Feel it in the soles of your feet?
Press your cheek against the soil.

That sound you hear is the creak
and groan of flame
becoming stone. The children

have escaped and are rampaging across
the land. There is nothing
to do but wait to see which dies first,

their anger, their interest, or them.
Relax, we are indeed
still in the seventh day. When the mail

drops through the slot, everyone stops
talking and turns,
giving the conversation over

to silence, as one does on entering
a library, a bunker,
a tomb. Let us build

only with porcelain and spiderweb,
let's hang the rice-paper moon
from a lute string, mount the yolk of sun

on a glass pedestal, perforate the night
with the hatpins of glorious ladies
and look down on our delicate world.

The uneasiness is settling,
an entropy of mood;
things are looking up, and not in fear.

The paper airplanes are flying again,
the zeppelins are brightly coloured
and say *Happy New Year* on the side,

the autos crashing into one another
on the street only bounce
away and run off cometing sparks.

Somewhere a train runs
on time. That tanker
that ran aground on the coral reef

was empty; there are children swimming
with penguins in the shelter
its bulk provides from the tireless surf.

Do yourself a quick favour:
look around. All the exits
are choked with the bodies of those

who realized it was time to flee
before you. There's nothing
wrong with spinning out of control

when, for once, you've been given
                              enough space.

Dust

Regardless, the trees will still stretch out
from their wrinkled sleep,
will hang a canopy of limp hands. Look down

that quiet lane where the branches make
an arch and say what you see:
far enough down, any road becomes a street

or ends in the wild. The fireflies are being
mistaken for stars again
by the drunkard stumbling home alone

through the woods. When the water runs
brown from the tap
you would do better to wash the dust

from your eyes with the gin left pooled
in this broken bottle.
Every campfire arrayed outside

these city walls is the seventh tongue
of an angry god. If only
life, having formed so suddenly

in that primordial moment a billion years gone,
had done so five minutes sooner,
there would still be time enough left

to figure out how to avoid all this. Look up
at the wall-to-wall sky
just barely visible through the foliage,

ask yourself how perpetuity
is shaping up.
Likely it's less eternal than you hoped.

CRANE

By which road did they come,
the one through the jungle
or the one through the desert?

The one through the mountain pass.
Ah, it is open again?
It is open to them. All roads are open

to them? They don't require roads.
They seldom use them?
They float above all roads, they move

as the crane flies; all roads lead
somewhere and, with a little
thought, here could be somewhere.

By which road did they leave,
the one through the mountain pass
or the coastal highway? Again,

even in leaving, they use no roads.
Their steeds don't touch the ground?
They own no horses, sit no saddle.

Then why must our ears be covered
at the thunder of their approach?
They are as silent as the stars. Then why

do our ears ring with the detonation
of their departure? It is your lot.
What then is this confusion we see

playing itself out on the horizon?
What you see roiling there is
smoke not clouds, sunset not flame.

ACKNOWLEDGEMENTS

The author thanks the following for their advice on certain poems: Jonathan Bennett, Peter Buck, Anita Chong, Peter Darbyshire, Joelle Hann, Adam Jacob Levin, Ellen Seligman, Silas White.

The author extends extra thanks to Ailsa Craig and A.F. Moritz, who edited the book for the author and McClelland & Stewart respectively.

The writing of this book was made possible by the generosity of the Canada Council for the Arts.

Some of these poems were first published, often in different form, in the following publications: in Australia, *Jacket*; in Canada, *The Capilano Review, Descant, Globe and Mail, The Literary Review of Canada, Maisonneuve*; in the United States, *LaPetiteZine, The Painted Bride Quarterly, Poetry After 9/11: An Anthology of New York Poets, Slope*.

INDEX OF TITLES